guide to ST. PETER'S
BASILICA

PHOTOS AND TEXT BY GIANFRANCO CRIMI

E

Futura Edizioni

Cover photo: Nave and Baldachin
Back cover: The Universal Judgement
Second cover: The statue of St. Peter before the Basilica
Third cover: The Creation of Man

Drawings by Angela Foschini
Translation from the Italian by Johanna Lipford

© 2012 FUTURA EDIZIONI
e-mail: futured@tiscali.it
http://web.tiscali.it/futuraedizioni
00156 Roma
Via Costantino Mortati, 130
Tel. 06.41218931
Fax 1786004690

Summary

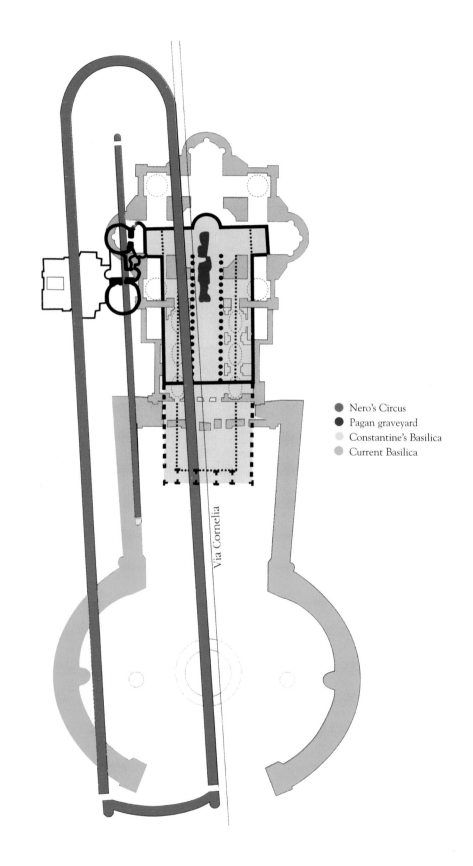

● Nero's Circus
● Pagan graveyard
● Constantine's Basilica
● Current Basilica

Via Cornelia

Its history

The basilica's origins begin with the great fire in 64 BC, when the emperor Nero, unjustly suspected of having ordered it, blamed it on the Christians, these being members of a new religious sect. A violent persecution followed, Christians being martyred in Nero's circus at the foot of Vatican hill, where the basilica now stands. Among those martyrs was the apostle Peter, who was buried in a necropolis nearby. That tomb became the subject of veneration and was enlarged to form an aedicula or funeral chapel around 160, as the imperial stamps impressed on the bricks bear witness. The archaeological digs that began in 1939 laid bare a red plastered wall, on which among the various graffiti was found a legend: *Petr en*. This, adding a few letters cancelled by time, becomes the Greek *Petros eni*, whose translation is «Peter is here».

Reconstruction of St. Peter's tomb. **Drawing by Angela Foschini**

A model of Costantine's basilica

After his victory at the Milvian bridge over Maxentius, the emperor Constantine decided, in agreement with pope Sylvester I, to build right at that spot a large basilica. To do this he took on considerable excavations of the Vatican hill and in 326 it was consecrated. It was finished in 349 by Constant, son of Constantine, and had a nave and four aisles, preceded by a four-sided portico accessed from a thirty-five step stairway. It stood there for twelve centuries, until, owing to the sacking it had undergone while it was abandoned during the Avignon period, pope Nicholas V Parentucelli (1447-1455), convinced that it was no longer possible to restore it, commissioned Leon Battista Alberti to work up a design for a new basilica. He appointed Bernardo Gamberelli, called *il Rossellino*, works director. The enterprise had hardly begun when it stopped owing to the pope's sudden death. His successors went ahead with little conviction, until Julius II Della Rovere gave the project a new impulse by assigning the design to architect Donato Bramante, who opted for a church with a Greek cross plan, that is with the arms all the same length. Bramante saw to the construction of the four powerful columns with huge arches, assigned to supporting the great dome. To build them he was not sparing in demolishing portions of the old basilica, unleashing polemics that included among his critics Michael Angelo and Erasmus of Rotterdam. From that time he was nicknamed "*maestro ruinante*" (the maestro of ruination). This design never saw the light owing to the deaths of both the pope and the architect.

Various artists followed, among them Giuliano da Sangallo, Raffaello Sanzio, Giocondo da Verona, Baldassarre Peruzzi and Antonio da Sangallo. This last-named had a wood model of his design made, which is still conserved in the church.

Façade and portico of Constantine's basilica.
Drawing by Angela Foschini

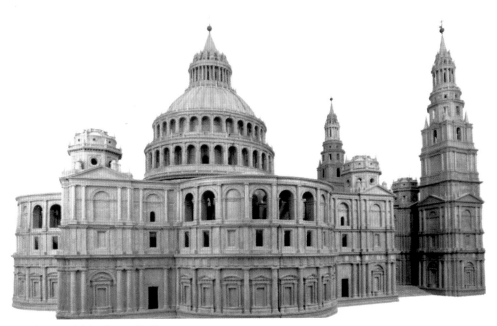

Wooden model by Sangallo the younger

Paul III Farnese confirmed the commission to Sangallo, among the various works he superintended, he raised the elevation of the flooring, thus permitting the possibility of the construction, afterward, of the Grottos. but the latter's death in 1546 led him to call on the by now seventy-year-old Michael Angelo, he being assigned the commission as architect-in-chief of the construction of St. Peter's. He abandoned Sangallo's design and went back to Bramante's, simplifying it. Michael Angelo strengthened the pylons that were to support the dome, which itself became the focus of the design, taking his inspiration for it from the dual spherical vault designed by Filippo Brunelleschi for the church of *Santa Maria del Fiore* in Florence. On his death the work had arrived at the drum of the dome and his place was taken by Pirro Ligorio, who was flanked by Jacopo Barozzi called il Vignola. There followed Giacomo Della Porta, one of Michael Angelo's students, who built the dome from 1588 to 1590. He preferred the raised arch solution, increasing the dome's height by seven meters over that conceived by Michael Angelo, and inserted reinforcing chains at the base of the drum.

The new pope, Paul V, and his cardinals took on the choice of the basilica's definitive form. The Greek cross was forsaken, as was envisioned by Bramante's design, taken back up by Michael Angelo, which would have represented a single whole mass between dome and front, in favour of the Latin

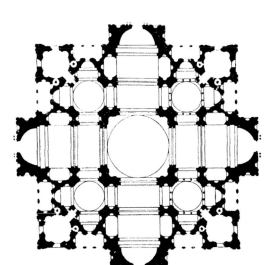

Greek cross plan, according to Bramante's design

The facade of the model
by Antonio da Sangallo

cross (the vertical is longer). Renaissance taste was changing. New liturgical requirements that permitted holding processions within the basilica, and the desire to receive all the faithful who crowded the services and the worship ceremonies, favoured the choice of this last-named. It was not easy to make since the works had already gone considerably ahead and the project could not be changed entirely, since its western end and the dome were almost complete. The only logical possibility was to lengthen its eastern end, by adding three chapels per side beyond the point where Michael Angelo had decided that the basilica must end.

Carlo Maderno was appointed the new architect of St Peter's Building, in 1603. His design, among the many presented by other architects, was chosen for the completion of the basilica and in 1608 the works began. At his side worked one of his distant relatives, he too in Rome, Francesco Castelli, called Borromini, who from being a simple stone-dresser became his closest coworker, as well as an architect of genius.

The outside work having been completed, that involving the decoration and the furnishings of the basilica's interior began. One of the most demanding was the construction of the baldachin. The idea came to Paul V, who, wishing to forsake the classical tradition of the ciborium (or baldachin), asked Maderno to build a baldachin and to prepare a model of it. At first he thought to build it of wood, but the arrival of the new pope, Urban VIII Barberini, brought with it some vexations. The pope had no great enthusiasm for Maderno, since as cardinal he had opposed the Latin cross design. Furthermore tastes were changing and Maderno was certainly not one of their new interpreters.

Anyway, he confirmed him as architect of the Building, not wishing to be deprived of his deep knowledge of the basilica and its construction. He did decide, however, thus bringing Maderno a great disappointment, to take from him

Presentation of Michael Angelo's design to Pope Paul III, Farnese

the design of the baldachin, assigning it instead to Bernini, who would become his consultant. On Maderno's death in 1629, Urban VIII appointed, at the age of just thirty years, Gian Lorenzo Bernini architect of the Reverend Building of St. Peter's. The project went ahead with the cooperation of Francesco Borromini from 1624 through 1633. It was decided to create the twisted gilded-bronze columns with at their tops a statue of the risen Christ on a pedestal. This very stagy solution, if scantly attentive to feasibility and to statics calculations, was changed, at Borromini's suggestion, since the statue of Christ would have been too heavy for the end structures of the top of the baldachin.

Borromini designed the four dolphin-spine structures and decided to replace the statue with a globe holding up a cross. Borromini's experience and technical competence, whether in the field of architecture or in the casting of bronze,

Model of the dome, made by Michael Angel

were superior to Bernini's. He was a very able and precocious sculptor, a great artist, but not as yet master of the subject of architecture, as he would become later on. For this reason he convinced Borromini to see to the basilica's and Barberini Palace's technical questions, the latter being another order received from the pope. He promised that he would give him a worthy recompense for all the work, but when it came down to paying he gave him nothing, whether in money or in recognition of the work done, attributing to himself the merits and the pope's recognition. This attitude brought about a break in their relations, one never healed, and Borromini abandoned the St Peter's construction yard as well as that of the Barberini Palace.

Gian Lorenzo Bernini went on with his work as architect of the basilica, but two decades later he ran into his most serious professional misfortune, which for a period of time cancelled him from Rome's artistic firmament.

Owing to an excess of self confidence, and not considering the opinion of any other architect, he decided to ignore Maderno's previous negative experience and went ahead with an expensive and imposing project involving two three-storey campaniles. The appearance of cracks in the façade and in the foundations provoked worries such as to impose an immediate suspension of the

Borromini's study for the Basilica baldachin

job. The new pope, Innocent X Pamphili, appointed a commission of eight cardinals to ascertain the responsibility for this and reports were requested of several architects, among whom Borromini, who wrote that the foundations had been designed to support a single floor above the façade and not a tower three times higher and six times heavier. Despite the commission's having requested advice from the best architects – and sought a solution convenient for everyone – Innocent X laid it down that everything built beyond the apostles on the terrace was to be razed. Still more surprising was the procedure for the confiscation of Bernini's property: 30,000 scudos were demanded as repayment for the damage undergone by the Congregation. Carlo Fontana and Luigi Vanvitelli followed, their job to solve a serious problem involving cracks found in the dome.

The square

T he construction of the square was desired by pope Alexander VII, in order that the more solemn functions involving participation by large numbers of the faithful could be held. He encharged Gian Lorenzo Bernini, who thought of an elliptical-plan colonnade that wrapped the square in an embrace - a definite allegorical intention desired by Bernini. The arms

are 120 meters long and seventeen wide; the one to the left is called Charlemagne, and the one to the right Constantine, and from it access is had to the Vatican Palace through the grand staircase.

Atop it are 140 statues depicting the defenders of the faith, the founders of religious orders, popes, bishops, Doctors of the Church, saints and martyrs.

△
◁

The grand staircase

St. Peter's square at sunset

Bernini's fountain on the left
side of the square

Detail of Bernini's fountain,
the sculptured arms are of Clement X

The right fountain was placed by Innocent VIII in 1490, and reworked by Maderno in 1614. To its left, Bernini had an almost identical fountain set, symmetrically about the obelisk; it was unveiled in 1675.

Detail of Maderno's fountain,
the sculptured arms are of Paul V

Maderno's fountain, on the right side
of the square

Carlo Fontana. Hauling the obelisk
to St. Peter's square

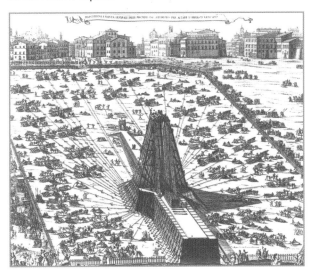

The 25-meter-high red granite obelisk was transported by the emperor Caligula from Heliopolis Egypt, and set down in his circus, which later became Nero's. In 1586 Sixtus V commissioned architect Domenico Fontana to place it where we see it today. The enterprise, arduous from an engineering standpoint, took four months and involved the labor of a thousand men, four thousand pounds of hemp rope and iron, 140 horses and forty-four winches.

Detail of the base of the obelisk with the ancient Roman inscriptions dedicated to «divo Augusto» and «divo Tiberio»

Between obelisk and fountains are two porphyry granite disks that mark the foci of the ellipse. From them the exact alignments of the four files of 284 columns can be observed.

The four street lamps, designed by Antonio Sarti, were placed by Pius IX in 1854. So too were the statues of St. Peter, by Giuseppe De Fabris and of St. Paul, by Adamo Tadolini, originally conceived for St. Paul's basilica. Recently a small memorial tablet was inset in the pavement to mark the point where John Paul II was shot in 1981.

The facade

I t is the work of Carlo Maderno, who had however the constraint of the already-erected side walls, to Michael Angelo's design. High 45.50 meters and 117.70 meters long, it is scanned by eight 27 meter columns and four pilaster strips in Corinthian style that sustain the cornice. On the balustrade are thirteen statues representing Christ the Redeemer, St. John Baptist, and eleven apostles.

The statues of the baluster

The facade

The loggia of blessings

The consignment of the Keys by Ambrogio Buonvicino

At the center is the Loggia of the Benedictions, so called because from here the pope comes out to impart his *Urbi et orbi* blessing, which is to say, of the city and to the world. Below the loggia is the bas-relief by Ambrogio Buonvicino, depicting the Consignment of the keys.

Originally, to the sides two campaniles were to stand, to lighten the horizontal extension of the façade but Maderno, when the façade had not as yet reached its full height, had to interrupt the work because the underlying soil had settled. Twenty years afterward, without taking account of Maderno's difficulties, Gian Lorenzo Bernini saw the project that called once again for the contruction of the campaniles approved. After the start of the work worrisome statics problems showed up in the foundations, and this meant suspending the job and wrecking what has been built. Of those constructions there remain the large arched passageways, which seem to be part of the structure, while the design would have had them detached. The legend indicates 1612 as the year the job was concluded, but it went ahead another two years to finish the cornice and to place the statues on the balustrade. Between 1786 and 1790 the two mosaic-dial clocks designed by Giuseppe Valadier were installed.

Clock, left

Clock, right

The atrium

T he atrium too is the work of Carlo Maderno, who was architect of the Reverend Construction of St. Peter's for twenty-six years. The vault is decorated with stuccoes designed by Giovan Battista Ricci da Novara, which narrate the history of apostles Peter and Paul. To the sides of the lunettes thirty-one statues depict the first martyred popes.

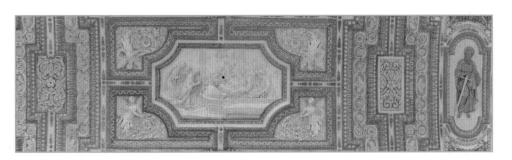

Costantine

Above, on the cornice overlooking the central door, can be seen the mosaic of the Navicella (small boat), executed by Giotto in 1300 for cardinal Stefaneschi, whose portrait is below to the right. It was then recomposed here, after further shiftings around, for the Jubilee year of 1675; a few parts of Giotto's original still remain.

Charlemagne

To the right we see an equestrian statue depicting Constantine, executed by Bernini and placed here at the start of the grand staircase on October 30th 1670, at the behest of Clement X Altieri. On the left another is counterposed, depicting Charlemagne, Holy Roman Emperor. It was commissioned by Clement XI to Agostino Cornacchini (1686-1784) and sculpted from a single block of Carrara marble. It was placed on March 30th of Jubilee year 1725.

The doors

The oldest is the central one, commissioned by pope Eugene IV Condulmer to Antonio Averulino, called Filarete.

The highest bays depict Christ the Redeemer and the Virgin; St. Paul and St. Peter consigning the keys to a kneeling Eugene IV; the judgement and beheading of St. Paul; the saint appearing to Plautilla and the crucifixion of St. Peter.

St. Peter consigns the Keys to pope Eugene IV

Crucifixion of St. Peter

Martyrdom of St. Paul

The author's bizarre signature: the maestro on horseback preceded by his aides and disciples

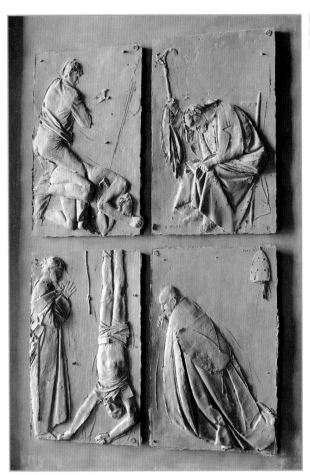

Detail of the Door of Death,
in which is portrayed,
in the last panel, John XXIII

The cardinals render homage
to John XXIII
▷

Giacomo Manzù's signature,
impressed on the back
of the door

The first door to the left, called of Death because funeral cortèges issued from it, is the work of Giacomo Manzù (1908-1991). He executed it between 1961 and 1964 to a commission by pope John XXIII (1958-1963), his fellow townsman, who is also depicted in it; it deals in fact with the theme of death. In the rear part are shown the cardinals taking part in Vatican Council II, and among them Lauran Rugambwe, first black cardinal created by him. The artist's signature can be seen on the imprint of the open hand. John XXIII did not see it finished and it was unveiled by Paul VI on September 28th 1964.

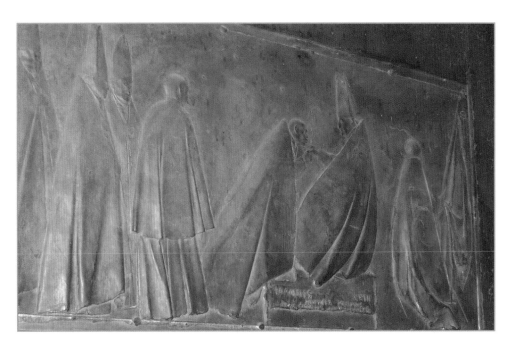

The second door, called of Good and Evil, is the work of Luciano Minguzzi and was consecrated on September 26th 1977, for Paul VI's eightieth birthday. The left leaf shows episodes referring to Evil. Good occupies the one to the right.

Detail of the Door of Good and Evil, by Luciano Minguzzi

The fourth, of the Seven Sacraments, is by Venanzio Crocetti and was unveiled by Paul VI on September 14th 1965.

The Holy Door

23

Jesus promises salvation to the thief who invokes it

The last, the Holy Door, by Vico Consorti, deals with the theme of salvation. It was placed in 1949 and the Swiss cardinal Francesco Von Streng donated, on behalf of Swiss Catholics, the bronze leaves as thanks for having preserved his country from the last world conflict.

The panels depict, beginning above to the left:

1) The cherub at the gates of Paradise.
2) Eve being chased from Paradise.
3) Mary, at the Annunciation.
4) The angel of the Annunciation.
5) The baptism of Jesus.
6) The lost sheep.
7) The merciful father.
8) The healing of the paralytic.
9) The sinning woman pardoned.
10) The duty to pardon.
11) Peter's denial.
12) Paradise to a thief.
13) The appearance to Thomas.
14) The appearance of the Risen Jesus in the Cenacle.
15) The appearance of the Risen Jesus to Saul.
16) The opening of the Holy Door

Jesus unhorses Paul

The nave

The nave

In the nave the attention is at once attracted by the two holy water fonts, which give an idea of the basilica's proportions, since they are two meters high. They were executed in 1725 by Agostino Cornacchini and Francesco Moderati (the left one) and by Giuseppe Lironi and Giovan Batista de' Rossi (the one to the right).

A little farther ahead from the central door a huge disk of red porphyry can be seen on the floor. It comes from the old basilica, where it was located near the high altar. On it Charlemagne received the crown of the Holy Roman Empire, from the hands of pope Leo III, on Christmas Eve in 800. Going ahead and observing the floor, the measurements of the fifteen largest churches in the world can be seen, shown in letters of bronze.

The Nave

Michael Angelo's design for the arms of the cross called for no decoration, the unitariness of the design being left only to the lines and to the architectural elements. But the change in design that lengthened the nave rendered the basilica rather bare, making for a feeling of coldness and excessive severity.

Innocent X assigned the decoration of the nave and aisles to Gian Lorenzo Bernini, who made use of a good forty-one workers for its execution. On the flooring, the great medallion with the dove depicts the pope's heraldic arms. On the columns, the tondos held up by putti depict the first fifty-six popes martyred: from St. Peter through Benedict I (575-579). At the center, another pair of putti hold up the symbols of papal authority: the keys, tiara and books.

The Nave. the arms of Innocent X

The putti that hold up
the tondos of the popes,
the keys and the tiara

Allegories of the Virtues: Faith

Between 1647 and 1649 Bernini began too the decoration of the great arches, having six-meter-tall statues depicting the virtues sculpted. Between 1714 and 1718 Lorenzo Ottoni completed the project with new allegories, the total number reaching 28.

The ceiling is gilded stucco, and the arms are Pius VI's.

Allegory of the Virtues   Heraldic arms of Pius VI

St. Francis,
sculpted by
Carlo Monaldi

St. Filippo Neri,
sculpted by
Giovan Battista Maini

On the great columns, between the pilaster strips, open two series of niches that contain 39 statues depicting the founders of religious orders and congregations, placed there beginning from 1706.

St. Norbert,
sculpted by
Pietro Bracci

St. Domenic Guzman, sculpted in 1706 by Pierre Legros

St. Vincent De Paul,
sculpted by Pietro Bracci

St. Elia, sculpted by
Agostino Cornacchini

Jean-Baptiste de la Salle

St. Bruno

St. Camillo de Lellis

St. Francesca Cabrini

St. Benedetto da Norcia

St. Ignacio de Loyola

St. Pietro d'Alcantara

St. Peter

Going on, to the right we see the bronze statue of St. Peter, attributed to Arnolfo di Cambio (1245-1310). Careful study of the technique and of the alloy confirms its compatibility with the techniques of that age. The veneration this statues enjoys is brought out by the wear undergone by the tip of the foot, kissed or stroked by the faithful.

Marble balustrade with the 89 flames in gilded bronze cornucopias

We now have before us the great altar of the Confession, built on the plumb line to the sepulchre of St. Peter. It is delimited by a marble balustrade where 89 flames in gilt bronze cornucopias permanently burn, designed by Mattia de' Rossi. Two flights of stairs lead down to a room richly decorated with marbles, with at its center a bronze railing, executed by Nicolas Cordier and Onorio Fanelli, and two statues of St. Peter and St. Paul, the work of Ambrogio Buonvicino, gilded and fused by Biagio de' Giusti. This is the level of the basilica of Constantine's times. Here is the votive chapel below which lies the tomb of St. Peter and here was found the tablet with the Greek writing *Petros eni*. At the center is the niche of the palliums; these stoles, contained in a bronze case, are woven of the wool of lambs blessed during the feast of St. Agnes, embroidered with black crosses. The pope makes gifts of them each year to a few metropolitan archbishops.

The Baldachin, the altar of the Confession and the niche of the palliums

Niche of the palliums and mosaic from the 9th century

Detail of a putto on one of the four columns of the Baldachin

The ninth-century mosaic depicts the Saviour and is the only element of the old basilica that can still be found in its original place.

At the center we see the papal altar, carven from a huge block of marble that was found in the Forum of Nerva. It was consecrated by Clement VIII on June 26th 1594 and on its interior is the altar of Callisto II of 1123. It is surmounted by the splendid bronze baldachin by Gian Lorenzo Bernini, commissioned to him by Urban VIII. He worked on it from 1624 to 1633, using 623 quintals of metal. The four spiral columns ornamented by olive branches and cherubim bear on four marble pedestals, at the center of which is sculpted a maternity sequence: the bees are the symbol of the Barberini family, from which Urban VIII sprang. Four angels surmount the baldachin, the work of Francois Duquesnoy, Andrea Bolgi and Giuliano Finelli. Another eight smaller ones hold up the symbols of the pope: the keys and the tiara, the book and the sword.

Over the whole thing dominates the cross resting on the globe. Even though inserted in this space it is hard to believe its height: 29 meters, that of the Farnese palace. The imposingness of the work did not evade criticism, in particular the way in which Urban VIII found the considerable amounts of bronze necessary. He took the ribs off the dome and the same amount he had come from Venice and Livorno. Since it was still not enough he did not hesitate to take the cramps from the atrium of the Pantheon. All this inspired Pasquino, the famous talking statue, to make the well known phrase *Quod non fecerunt barbari, Barberini fecerunt* (what the barbarians didn't do, the Barberini did). Another eccentric consequence of this «donation» were two bell towers erected to the sides of the Pantheon and that, with grating irony the Roman people called «Bernini's ass ears». They were razed, to no one's regret, in 1883.

Putti with the tiara and the keys

The cross placed on the top of the Baldachin

Francesco Borromini

Gian Lorenzo Bernini

One of the four angels surmounting the Baldachin

This splendid structure is topped by its spectacular dome, which bears on four enormous columns 45 meters high, having a perimeter of 71 meters.

St. John

St. Matthew

St. Luke

The four 8.5-meter-diameter medallions depict the four evangelists: Matthew, Mark with the lion, executed by Cesare Nebbia and Paolo Rossetti; Luke with the bull and John with the eagle, executed by Giovanni de' Vecchi.

On the interior of the drum the Latin writing says «You are Peter and on this rock I shall build my Church, and I shall give you the keys to the kingdom of heaven».

St. Mark

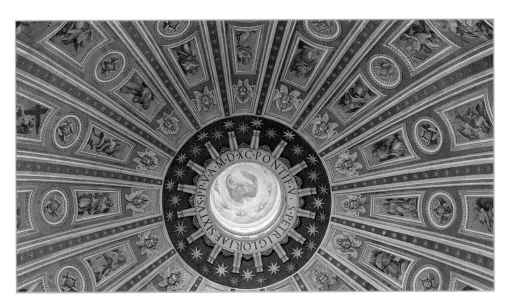

The dome is broken down into sixteen ribs, decorated with mosaics, whose figures depict, starting from the outside towards the interior:

1) Busts of the patriarchs and bishops.
2) Christ, the Virgin Mary, St. John Baptist, St. Paul and the apostles.
3) Angels with the instruments of Jesus' suffering.
4) Medallions with faces of seraphim and cherubim.
5) Angels looking at St. Peter's tomb.
6) Faces of winged seraphim, and in the lantern the figure of the Eternal Father.

The Latin writing on the ring that precedes the lantern: «to the glory of St. Peter, pope Sixtus V, in the year 1590, the fifth of his papacy» was added by Clement VIII Aldobrandini, in memory of his predecessor, who promoted the construction of the dome. Its decoration was assigned to Giuseppe Cesari, known as the Knight of Arpino (1568-1640), who designed the sixty-five cartoons. The figure on the interior of the small lantern was executed by Ranuccio Semprevivo between 1603 and 1604.

St. Helena

Detail of the column of the baldachin and loggia of St. Helena

In the four piers Bernini, who worked on them from 1628 through 1639, placed, at the behest of Urban VIII the four loggias of the relics. These are richly decorated balconies: in the upper part four angels, of whom two sustain a scroll; in the lower one two pilaster strips in the outer part act as frame for two spiral columns, coming from the ciborium of the old basilica, with in the

St. Veronica △ ▷

center a marble bas-relief inspired by the corresponding relic. The statues depict St. Helena, sculpted by Andrea Bolgi in 1646, whose signature can be seen on the base and along the hem of her dress; Veronica, work of Francesco Mochi, this too signed on the base.

Longines, sculpted by Bernini himself and the statue of St. Andrew, executed by Francois Duquenoy. This relic was donated by Paul VI in 1966, to the city of Patrasso where St. Andrew died.

St. Andrew

Turning towards the entry we find the Chapel of Piety, preceded by the rear of the Holy Door, above which stands a mosaic with a Sicilian jasper frame, St. Peter with keys and book, created by Fabio Cristofari to a design by Ciro Ferri.

Michael Angelo sculpted the Pietà on a block of Carrara marble, when he was just twenty-five years old, between 1498 and 1499, for the tomb of cardinal Jean Bilhéres de Lagraulas, ambassador of Charles VIII to pope Alexander VI. It was given various locations, until, in 1749, Benedict XIV Lambertini ordered that it be placed where we see it now. Its elliptical marble base is the work of Borromini. One curious fact about this statue is the signature, which was chiselled on the belt that crosses the breast. It is the only statue that Michael Angelo signed because, not as yet known, when the statue was first unveiled he, standing apart from the crowd, heard comments that attributed the work to Cristoforo Solari.

On May 20th 1971 a madman defaced it with h a m m e r blows and after its restora- tion it was protected by plate glass.

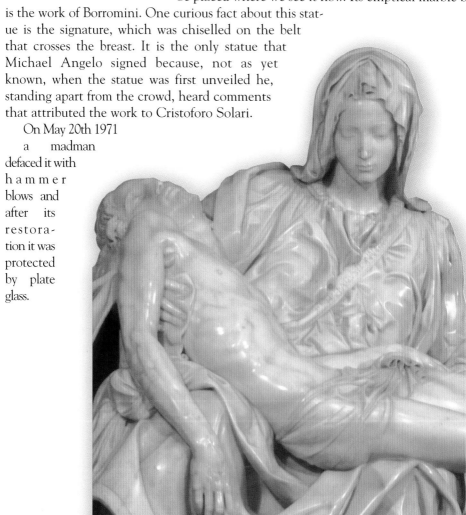

Monument to Christina of Sweden

Going ahead now, to the left we see the funeral monument of Queen Christina of Sweden, by Carlo Fontana (1634-1714), in gilded bronze. The three reliefs depict Christina renouncing the Swedish throne to convert to Catholicism; the scorn of the nobility (to the right); the faith that conquers heresy (left). She is buried in the Vatican Grottoes.

In front is the monument to Leo XII della Genga (1823-1829), work of Giuseppe de Fabris (1790-1860). The door leads to the chapel of the Relics or of the Crucifix, since it contains a wood crucifix attributed to the thirteenth-century Roman artist Pietro Cavallini.

Now we come upon the chapel of St. Sebastian (owing to the mosaic on the altar) executed by Pier Paolo Cristofari, to a design by Domenico Zampieri, called *Il Domenichino* (1581-1641). The two statues are modern: that of Pius XI (1922-39) was executed in 1949 by Francesco Nagni; that of Pius XII (1939-58) is by Francesco Messina, who executed it in 1964.

Mathilde di Canossa by Bernini

Pius XI

Pius XII

Moving on we see the funeral monument to Mathilde di Canossa, supporter of pope Gregory VII against the emperor Henry IV. Bernini, who personally sculpted the statue, took advantage of the contributions of numerous co-workers: Agostino Radi and Alessandro Loreti, who conceived its architecture; Giuseppe Balsimelli and Niccolò Sale roughed out the statue. The bas-relief represents Henry IV, kneeling before the pope on January 28th 1077, after having waited three days and three nights, and was sculpted by Stefano Speranza. The putti are the work of Bolgi (left) and of Luigi Bernini, brother of Gian Lorenzo (right). The putti with the crown and the arms were sculpted by Matteo Bonarelli, Lorenzo Flori and Andrea Bolgi (1605-1656).

Altar of St. Sebastian. The Blessed John Paul II was buried here

BEATVS
IOANNES PAVLVS PP.II

Facing is the baroque funeral monument of Innocent XII (1691-1700), work of 1746 of Francesco Della Valle and of Ferdinando Fuga. The two allegorical figures represent Justice and Charity (left).

Allegory of Charity

Now we enter the chapel of the Holy Sacrament, preceded by the very fine gate designed by Francesco Borromini (1599-1667). The stucco decorations of the vault depict episodes from the Old and New Testaments and are the work of Giovan Battista Ricci, to designs by Pietro Berrettini, called da Cortona (1596-1669). This artist is also the author of the altar panel - the only painting to be found in the basilica - depicting the Holy Trinity.

Altar of the chapel of the Most Holy

Detail of the tabernacle

Vault of the chapel of the Most Holy

Tabernacle by Bernini

On the altar can be admired the gilt bronze tabernacle, designed by Bernini, inspired by the little temple of Bramante in St. Peter in Montorio, with to its sides two angels. The mosaic on the right wall depicts the Ecstasy of St. Francis, by Il Domenichino.

Detail of the stuccoes on the vault

Monument of Gregory XIII

Going ahead, on the right we see the funeral monument of Gregory XIII (1572-1585), with the statues of Religion, holding in its hand the Bible and in the other a tablet with the writing «I know the works of Him and his faith». The other, depicting Strength, has the features of Minerva who is holding up the drape to show the bas-relief, which notes the calendar reform he wished, a shift from October 4th to October 15th of the earlier calendar going back to Julius Caesar. The winged dragon is the symbol of the arms of the Boncompagni family. The sculptures are the work of Camillo Rusconi (1658-1728) and the bas-relief was executed by Carlo Francesco Mellone.

Gregory XIII (portion)

At the mouth of the transept we find ourselves in the part of the basilica built to the design of Bramante and Michael Angelo. The nave is closed by the altar of St. Jerome, where we see reproduced in mosaic the famous painting of *Il Domenichino*, in which the saint takes his last communion, with beside him St. Paola intent on kissing his hand.

St. Jerome's Altar

On view below the altar is the body of John XXIII, proclaimed blessed and transported here on June 4th 2001.

The Madonna of Succour

Now we are in the Gregorian chapel, started by Michael Angelo, continued by Vignola and on his death, in 1573, brought to a close by Giacomo Della Porta. On the back wall the altar of the Madonna of Succour, a twelfth-century fresco, framed by elegant marble decorations and splendid African marble columns, the work of Girolamo Muziano (1528-1592).

The fresco, present too in the first basilica, was transferred here in 1578 by Gregorio XIII, the pope to whom we owe the choice of the mosaic transposition, preferred to the fresco. To the right is the monument to Gregorio XVI Cappellari (1831-1846), sculpted by Luigi Amici in 1854. the other altar is of St. Basil Magnus, by Pietro Subleyras (1699-1749), shown while he is celebrating the Mass of the Epiphany of 732: he is so absorbed that he is not aware of the presence of the emperor Valente.

Monument to Gregory XVI

Altar of St. Basil the Great

The right transept

I n the passage to the transept, to the right, the tomb of Benedict XIV Lambertini, by Pietro Bracci (1700-1733); his is also the allegorical statue of Wisdom, while that of Disinterest is by his pupil Gaspare Sibilia.

In the transept, along the curve of the apse, the altar with the mosaic of St. Wenceslaus, king of Bohemia, from the painting by Cesare Caroselli; the martyrdom of saints Processo and Martiniano, Peter's jailors in the Mamertine prison, to a design by Jean de Boulogne (1594-1632), called Giambologna; and the martyrdom of St. Erasmus by Nicholas Poussin (1594-1632). The vault was decorated by Luigi Vanvitelli, with stuccoes modelled by Giovan Battista Maini.

Monument to Benedict XIV

St. Wenceslau

Martyrdom of St. Erasmus

Martyrdom of Sts. Processo and Martiniano

Monument to Clement XIII

Having passed the transept, on the right is the funeral monument to Clement XIII Rezzonico, by Antonio Canova (1757-1822), which introduces the Neoclassical style into the basilica. To the left the statue of Religion and to the right The Genius of Death, which is extinguishing the torch of life. At its feet two particularly realistic lions in travertine marble, guarding the sepulchre. They were studied from life in the royal palace of Caserta, where two live lions were kept. On the urn, in relief, the figures of Charity and of Hope.

The Genius of Death

Altar of the Small Boat

To the left, the della Navicella (small boat) altar, showing St. Peter about to sink into the waters of the lake of Galilee, from the original by Giovanni Lanfranco, transposed into mosaic by Pietro Paolo Cristofari in 1720.

Vault of the chapel of St. Michael Archangel

St. Michael Archangel

St. Petronilla

We now enter the chapel of St. Michael Archangel and on the altar is the mosaic from the original by Guido Reni (1575-1642); on the altar in front is St. Petronilla, a mosaic by Pier Paolo Cristofari, from the original by Giovan Francesco Barbieri, called *Il Guercino* (1590-1666), currently in the Capitoline painting gallery.

St. Peter raising Tabitha from the dead

Detail of the stuccoes by Giovan Battista Maini

In the passage towards the apse we note the tomb of Clement X Altieri, executed to a design by Mattia de' Rossi (1637-1695). The statue of the pope was sculpted by Ercole Ferrata; the one of Clemency is by Giuseppe Mazzuoli; the statue of Beneficence (right) by Lazzaro Morelli. In the base is reproduced the opening of the Holy Door in the 1675 Jubilee, by Leonardo Reti. Tradition has it that the personage who holds the pope's mantel is cardinal Paluzzi, his grandson; while the personage kneeling with the tray in his hands is de' Rossi himself.

To the left is the altar with the reproduction of the painting by Placido Costanzi (1702-1759), St. Peter resuscitating Tabitha.

The apse

G ian Lorenzo Bernini's considerable Baroque imagination furnishes here a proof of his scenographic ability. Alexander VII commissioned him to construct a monument that would exalt an ancient throne, wooden with ivory insets, which legend told had belonged to Peter when he was preaching in Rome. In fact it is a throne from the ninth century, which it is supposed was brought to Rome by Charles the Bald when he was crowned in the basilica by John VIII in 875. Thus Bernini conceived this case in the form of a throne, which holds the throne on its interior. The solemn unveiling took place on January 17th 1666.

Over the chair two angels support tiara and the keys, symbols of the authority of the pontefice.

The throne of St. Peter

The doctors of the Latin and Greek church

The consignment of the keys

The crucifixion of St. Peter

The gilded bronze statues, 5.35 meters high, depict the Doctors of the Church: St. Athanasius and St. John Chrysostom; the internal statues, the Doctors of the Greek Church; those outside, St. Ambrose and St. Augustine, of the Roman Church.

Above the throne two angels hold up the tiara and the keys, symbols of the pope's authority. The whole is dominated by the fantastic *Gloria* in gilt stucco, where angels and putti look out from clouds and act as frame to the alabaster window with the dove, symbol of the Holy Spirit. This symbology expresses a theological concept: the Eastern Church and the Western Church are united in the Catholic Church, and both render homage to Peter's Throne. The vault is decorated with stuccoes designed by Vanvitelli and executed by Giovan Battista Maini: in the three medallions are depicted the consignment of the keys, the crucifixion of Peter and the beheading of St. Paul.

The Gloria and the Holy Spirit

On the right the funeral monument to Urban VIII Barberini (1623-1644), in bronze with gold highlights, designed by Bernini in 1627 and finished in 1646. Above the sarcophagus Death is depicted, writing on a parchment the name of the pope and in the leaves below the initials of the popes who preceded him: the G of Gregory XV and the P of Paul V, more faded. At the sides, in Carrara marble, Justice (right) and Charity.

Allegory of Justice

Allegory of Charity

The other funeral monument is Paul III's (1534-1549), the first to be erected in the basilica, conceived by Guglielmo Della Porta (1515-1577), commissioned by his nephew, cardinal Alessandro Farnese. At first the project called for eight statues, but only four were sculpted and two of them ended up in Palazzo Farnese. The two statues represent Justice and Prudence.

It is supposed that the former depicts the pope's sister, Giulia Farnese, whose nude was then covered with a metal mantle in 1595, at the behest of Clement VIII. The latter is supposed to portray the mother, Govannella Caetani. The architectural scheme takes up Michael Angelo's for the Medici tombs in the church of St. Laurence in Florence.

Allegories of Justice and Prudence

In the following passage is the sepulchre of Alexander VIII Ottoboni (1689-1691), to a design by Arrigo di San Martino; it was executed in bronze by Giuseppe Bertosi. The statues of Religion and of Prudence are by Angelo De' Rossi and the bas-relief depicts the canonization of five saints.

Saint Peter healing the paralytic

Marble altar panel depicting St. Leo the Great

We are now in the chapel of the Colonna and to the right we see the altar with the relics of St. Leo the Great (440-461), with its grand marble panel sculpted by Alessandro Algardi (1602-1656), depicting the pope's meeting with Attila, king of the Huns. The work was executed in five blocks of marble.

The Madonna of the column

The altar of the Madonna of the Column takes its name from a fresco of the Madonna painted on a column of the old basilica. Paul V had it moved here in 1607 and Paul VI , in 1964, at the conclusion of the third session of the Vatican Council II, honoured it with the title of *Mater Ecclesiae* (Mother of the Church). John Paul II had a copy of it placed on the outside of the Vatican Palace.

In the passage to the transept, the funeral monument of Alexander VII Chigi (1655-1667), which portrays the pope in prayer, while Death suddenly appears with its hourglass, announcing the expiry of the time of his life. The head was sculpted by Bernini. The statues in the foreground, Charity and Truth, were sculpted by Giuseppe Mazzuoli and by Lazzaro Morelli. In the background Prudence and Justice, sculpted by Giulio Cartari and by L. Balestri. To the left the altar with the Sacred Heart of Jesus, by Carlo Muccioli.

Funeral monument to Alexander VII

Charity and Prudence

Detail of the monument to Alexander VII

Truth and Justice

The Sacred Heart of Jesus

The hour-glass and Charity

The unbelief of St. Thomas

St. Joseph

The crucifixion of St. Peter

The punishment of Saphira

The three altars, beginning from the one to the right, depict the Unbelief of St. Thomas, by Vincenzo Carnuccini; St. Joseph, by Achille Funi; and the Crucifixion of St. Peter, from the original by Guido Reni. To the right the funeral monument of Pius VIII Castiglioni (1820-1823), work of Pietro Tenerani (1789-1869). Below it a door opens that leads to the sacristy and to the treasure.

On the left altar the Punishment of Sapphira, from the painting by Cristoforo Roncalli, called *Il Pomarancio* (1552-1626), itself conserved in the church of St. Mary of the Angels in Rome. We are now in the Clementine chapel, commissioned by pope Clement VIII Aldobrandini, whose arms stand out in the center of the floor. It was started by Michael Angelo and was brought to a finish by Giacomo Della Porta (1540-1602), on the occasion of the Jubilee of 1600.

Detail of the monument to Pius VIII

Monument Pius VIII

To the right, the monument in Neoclassical taste lying over the entrance to the sacristy is dedicated to Pius VIII, and was executed by Pietro Teherani in 1866. Behind the kneeling pope is the Christ, and to the sides are St. Peter and St. Paul. To the sides of the door are allegories of Prudence and Justice.

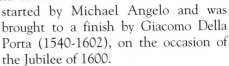
Sacristy.
List of the popes buried in the Basilica

73

The altar is dedicated to St. Gregory the Great (590-604). His remains are conserved in a sarcophagus under the altar. To this pope we owe the Gregorian chant and the evangelization of England. The mosaic is taken from the painting of 1625 by Andrea Sacchi (1599-1661). Several princes had requested precious relics of pope Gregory, who gave them a cloth wrapping a few relics. The princes judged them of low value and indignantly returned them. Gregory, after having prayed, had a knife brought him and he punctured the relics, to show how the blood flowed from them.

The mosaics in the dome were executed by Marcello Provenzale and Paolo Rossetti, to designs by *Il Pomarancio*.

In the left wall is inserted the funeral monument of Pius VII Chiaramonti

St. Leo the Great

(1800-1823), work of the Danish sculptor Bertel Thorvaldsen (1770-1844). This commission provoked ill feeling: both because he was a foreigner and most especially because he was a Protestant. The allegorical statues represent the Genius of Time and of History; Strength, clothed in a lion's skin and Wisdom, with the book and the owl.

Monument to Pius VII

Allegory of Strength and the
Genius of History

Monument to Pius VII:
allegorical depictions of the
Genius of Time and of
Wisdom with book and owl

Detail of the stuccoes
in the vault

Detail of the
stuccoes in
the vault of the
transept

Left aisle

On the left altar, the mosaic copy of Raphael's Transfiguration (1483-1520), his last work. The artist depicts two episodes narrated in the gospels of Mark and Matthew: the Transfiguration of Christ on Mount Tabor and the Healing of the youth possessed by the devil.

Leo XI

At the beginning of the aisle, to the right, the funeral monument of Leo XI de' Medici, by Alessandro Algardi (1595-1654), who sculpted the statue of the pope and the bas-relief of the urn. The figure of Magnanimity is by Ercole Ferrata; that of Liberality, which is pouring gold and jewels from a cornucopia, by Giuseppe Peroni. The writing on the scroll between a bunch of roses, *Sic Florvi* (it flowered so), alludes to the brevity of his papacy, which lasted only twenty-seven days.

ocent XI

To the left the monument to Innocent XI Odescalchi (1676-1689), the work of the French sculptor Stephan Monnot, whose signature is on the shield. To the sides the allegories of Faith and of Justice; in the bas-relief is noted the defeat of the Turks at Vienna in 1683, the work of Giovanni Sobiesky. In this battle the pope made his own contribution. The overall design is by Carlo Maratta (1625-1713).

With the chapel of the Choir begins the basilica with nave and two aisles, Maderno's design. The stuccoes were executed by Giovan Battista Ricci, while the altar mosaic, which depicts the Immaculate surrounded by angels, St. Francis, St. Antonio da Padova and John Crisostom, is taken from the painting by Pietro Bianchi (1694-1740).

The chapel of the choir

The wooden choir was commissioned by Urban VIII and executed under Maderno's supervision. The elegant railing is the work of Borromini, who on September 9th 1628, in his payment receipt, signed for the first time with this name, instead of his name at birth, which was Francesco Castelli.

The immaculate Madonna

Detail of the stuccoes in the vault

Detail of the stuccoes and of the Baroque organ

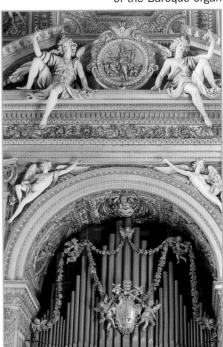

Monument to St. Pius X

In the passage between this chapel and the next, we see to the right the monument to St. Pius X (1904-1914), designed by architect Florestano Di Fausto and sculpted by Pier Enrico Astorri in 1923.

Detail of the bronze reliefs

◁   △

To the left the funeral monument to Innocent VIII Cybo (1484-1492), work of Antonio Pollaiolo (1431-1498), already present in the old basilica and transferred here in 1619.

The pope is depicted in the act of blessing and has in his left hand the lance of Longines, the relic donated to him by the Sultan Bajaset II. To the sides are depicted the four cardinal virtues: Prudence, Justice, Strength and Temperance. In the upper lunette the theological virtues: Faith, Hope and Charity. In the original placement the sarcophagus was above.

Monument to Innocent VIII

Detail of
Innocent VIII

Presentation of Maria
in the temple

There now follows the chapel of the Presentation, which takes its name from the painting by Giovan Francesco Romanelli, the Presentation of Maria at the Temple. Below the altar is conserved the body of St. Pius X. The chapel is decorated with mosaics to designs by Carlo Maratta. To the right the bronze monument for John XXIII Roncalli (1958-1963), work of Emilio Greco, who depicts him during a visit to the convicts in Regina Coeli prison. To the left the funeral monument of Benedict XV Della Chiesa, (1914-1922)sculpted by Pietro Canonica (1869-1959); thus too the bas-relief, in which the pope propitiates divine mercy for the horrors of war and Mary presents to a world in flames Jesus, prince of peace.

Monument of John XXIII

Monument of Benedict XV

Monument to Maria Clementina Sobiesky

Going ahead, on the right the monument to Maria Clementina Sobiesky (1702-1735), who died in Rome, granddaughter of John II, king of Poland.

In 1719 she married James III Stuart, pretender to the throne of England. The design was executed by Filippo Barigioni and the statue of Charity is the work of Pietro Bracci; the original portrait is by Ludwig Stern and was executed in mosaic by Pietro Paolo Cristofari.

Portrait of Clementina and the allegory of Charity

In front is the funeral stele of the monument to the Stuarts, executed by Antonio Canova, which depicts James III with his sons Charles Edward, count of Albany, and cardinal Henry Benedict, duke of York, bishop of Frascati and arch-priest of St. Peter's basilica.

James III   Cardinal Henry Benedict   Charles Edward

Details of the winged Geniuses

◁   ▽

The chapel of Baptism

The last chapel is of Baptism, designed by Carlo Fontana (1634-1714), with at its center the baptismal font in red porphyry, carved from the cover of the sarcophagus of Otto II, who died in Rome in 983 and was buried in the ancient basilica. The gilt-bronze cover was designed by Fontana and modelled by Giovanni Giardini. The altar panel, the Baptism of Jesus by John Baptist, conserved in St. Mary of the Angels, was transposed from a painting by Carlo Maratta. To the right a mosaic with St. Peter baptizing the centurion Cornelius, by Andrea Procaccini, of 1711. To the left Peter baptizing Processo and Martiniano, from a painting by Giuseppe Passeri.

Before the chapel, on the floor, the arms of John Paul II, unveiled on October 16th 1994.

Detail of one of the two angels with the terrestrial globe and the Trinity

The vatican grottoes

The Grottoes extend from three meters below the current level of the papal altar on to around one-half the nave. Niches, corridors, chapels and funeral monuments ramify on their interior; here too is also St. Peter chapel, and

Funeral monument of Boniface VIII

directly below it, in the underground necropolis, is the Apostle tomb.

Besides holding the tombs of a number of popes, the Grottoes also keep custody of historical memories and numerous works of art coming from the ancient basilica and from excavations in the necropolis. Among the various popes and other historical personages who expressed their wish to be buried nearby St. Peter tomb, we note: Gregory V (996-999), the emperor Otho III (who died in Rome in 983), Hadrian IV (1154-1159), the only English pope, Boniface VIII (1294-1303), who proclaimed the first holy year, Pius VI, who died a prisoner of the French in 1779, James III Stuart and his children, and Christina of Sweden (1626-1689). The last popes to be buried here were Benedict XV, Pius XI and Pius XII, John XXIII (who was moved to below the altar of St. Jerome), Paul VI, John Paul I.

Funeral monument of Callixtus III

Tomb of Benedict XV

First tomb of Johnn Paul II.

Monument of Pius VI,
started by Antonio Canova
and finished by Adamo Tadolini

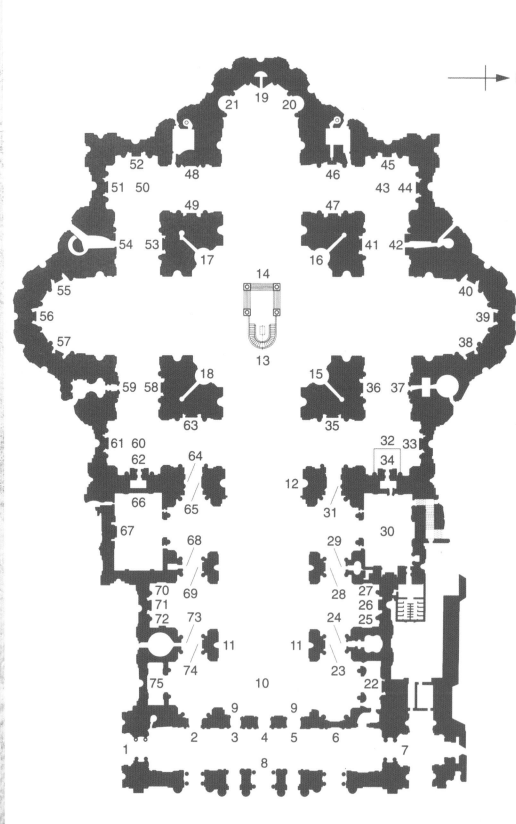

N

Map of St. Peter's

ATRIUM
1 Statue of Charlemagne
2 Door of Death
3 Door of Good and Evil
4 Filarete's door
5 Door of the Seven Sacraments
6 Holy door
7 Statue of Costantine
8 Mosaic of Navicella

THE NAVE
9 Clocks
10 Disc of red porphyry
11 Holy water fonts
12 Bronze statue of St. Peter
13 Chapel of confession
14 Papal altar and baldachin
15 Pillar of St. Longines
16 Pillar of St. Helena
17 Pillar of St. Veronica
18 Pillar of St. Andrew
19 St. Peter's throne
20 Monument to Urban VIII
21 Monument to Paul III

THE RIGHT AISLE
22 Chapel of piety
23 Monument of Christina of Sweden
24 Monument to Leon XII
25 Monument to Pius XI
26 Chapel of St. Sebastian
27 Monument to Pius XII
28 Monument to Mathilde of Canossa
29 Monument of Innocent XII
30 Chapel of the Holy Sacrament
31 Monument to Gregory XIII

RIGHT TRANSEPT
32 Gregorian chapel
33 Madonna of succour
34 Monument to Gregory XVI
35 Altar of St. Jerome
36 Altar of St. Basil Magnus

37 Monument to Benedict XIV
38 Altar of St. Wenceslaus
39 Altar of Saints Processo and Martiniano
40 Altar of St. Erasmus
41 Altar of the Navicella
42 Monument to Clement XIII
43 Chapel of St. Michael Archangel
44 Altar of St. Michael Archangel
45 Altar of St. Petronilla
46 Monument to Clement X
47 Altar of Tabitha

LEFT TRANSEPT
48 Monument to Alexander VIII
49 Altar of the paralytic
50 Chapel of the Madonna of the Column
51 Altar of the Madonna of the Column
52 Altar of St. Leo the Great
53 Altar of the Sacred Heart of Jesus
54 Monument to Alexander VII
55 Altar of St. Thomas
56 Altar of St. Joseph
57 Altar of the crucifixion of St. Peter
58 Altar of Punishment of Saphira
59 Monument to Pius VIII
60 Clementine chapel
61 Altar of St. Gregory the Great
62 Monument of Pius VII
63 Altar of the transfiguration

LEFT AISLE
64 Monument to Leo XI
65 Monument to Innocent XI
66 The chapel of the choir
67 Altar of the Immaculate Madonna
68 Monument to St. Pius X
69 Monument to Innocent VIII
70 Monument to John XXIII
71 Altar of the Presentation
72 Monument to Benedict XV
73 Monument to Maria Clementina Sobiesky
74 Monument to the Stuarts
75 The chapel of Baptism

The Sistine Chapel

The Sistine Chapel takes its name from pope Sixtus IV Della Rovere, who, following his fifteenth-century predecessors, wished to give back to Rome the most important monuments of Christianity after the Avignon episode and the civil struggles that had led to the city's abandonment and neglect. He assigned the project to Baccio Pontelli and Mino da Fiesole, his purpose to outfit the

View of the interior of the Sistine Chapel. In the foreground: Mino da Fiesole's transenna

The exterior
of the Sistine Chapel

Vatican with a sumptuous environment in which to worthily celebrate the most solemn liturgical ceremonies. The decoration of the walls engaged such painters as Pietro Perugino, Sandro Botticelli, Domenico Ghirlandaio, Cosimo Rosselli and Luca Signorelli. The presence of all these Florentine artists in Rome owed to Lorenzo de' Medici who, wishing to pursue a project that would reconcile him with Sixtus IV, Lorenzo himself involved in the plot of the Pazzi, where his brother Giuliano de' Medici had died, proposed sending these artists, thus too affirming Florence's artistic supremacy.

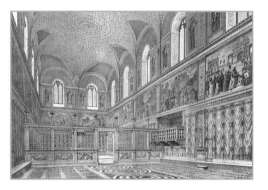

The Sistine Chapel's appearance, before Michael Angelo's operations

The vault originally represented a starry sky and had been painted by Pier Matteo d'Amelia, as is shown by a sixteenth-century design conserved in the Uffizi galleries. The work began in 1481 and ended the next year. In the Chapel there are works in marble such as the transenna, wrought by Mino da Fiesole, Andrea Bregno and Giovanni Dalmata, which served to separate the part reserved to the pope from that for the faithful. Then it was moved to provide greater space for the pope and his court. Following the flooring design, one can see where the transenna originally arrived. The choir, built by the same artists, served to host the choir singers, usually twelve of them, who accompanied the liturgical celebrations. Above the entrance

The Sistine Chapel's left wall

were the pope's arms, an oak tree with twelve gold acorns, of the Della Rovere family.

On August 5th 1483 Sixtus IV consecrated the chapel and dedicated it to the Assumption of the Virgin Mary.

God Dividing Light from Darkness.

Creation of the Sun and the Moon

Julius II Della Rovere (1503-1513), Sixtus IV's nephew, decided to completely redo the decoration, owing to the damage caused by problems of a statics nature concerning the Chapel, which brought about the opening of a long crack in the vault. Bramante, the Palace architect, was called, and he solved the problem by installing a number of chains in the room above the Chapel. The damage undergone by the paintings was so serious that Julius II decided to call Michael Angelo to assign to him the commission for a new decoration. On May 8th 1508 the artist signed the contract for creating twelve apostles in the pendentives and ornamental motifs in the rest.

God Separating Waters from the Land

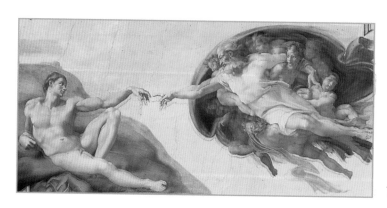

The Creation of Man

Michael Angelo, who deemed the project to be rather paltry, asked the pope for a free hand on a wholly new project, one of his own ideation.

With the help of theologians of the papal court, he conceived nine central scenes involving episodes from Genesis, with to the sides figures of nudes, prophets and sybils, the forefathers of Christ and in the four cor-

The Creation of Woman

The Originai Sin

ner pendentives episodes involving the saving of the people of Israel. The work of preparation: sketches, cartoons, surface preparations, took much time. As did the scaffolding on which he was to work. In fact Michael Angelo discarded that conceived by Bramante, since being suspended from the ceiling by cords, it would have left unaesthetic holes. Thus he

The Sacrifice of Noah

The Deluge

adapted one of them in use for the pour of the vaults. Having finished one-half of the vault, it was dismounted and moved. The artist therefore had the possibility of seeing from below the effect of the frescoes. The work was completed on October 31st 1512.

The Drunkennes of Noah

The Last Judgement

In 1533 Clement VII de' Medici (1523-1534), got into contact with Michael Angelo through the painter Sebastiano del Piombo. This latter on July 17th wrote him a letter prospecting for him the project of frescoing the Universal Judgement. The Florentine artist, after some hesitation, decided to accept the commission.

The work began in 1536, under the new pope Paolo III Farnese (1534-1549). The first stage of the work was to line the wall with a wall of inclined bricks so as to ensure that the least possible amount of dust was deposited. This involved the loss of the frescoes executed by Perugino on that wall. The first coat of the colour began to have mould problems, since the surface had remained wet too long owing to a mortar made up with lime and pozzolana that was too watery. Michael Angelo had to remove these parts and, together with a co-worker, Jacopo di Lazzaro, called the *Indaco* (indigo), they prepared a new mixture that dried more slowly but stood up to the mould.

During the work Michael Angelo had a dispute with cardinal Carafa, who accused him of immorality and obscenity owing to the nude figures with their genitals in view. The question culminated with a true censure campaign to have those nudes covered, considered not to be consonant with a papal chapel. Giorgio Vassari, painter and writer of the age, relates that among its detractors was Biagio da Cesena, the pope's master of ceremonies, who judged the frescoes worthy of a baths or a winehouse. Michael Angelo took his revenge by depicting him under the appearance of Minos, one of the judges of the Beyond in Greek mythology. At the master of ceremonies' remonstrance with the pope, this latter replied that his jurisdiction did not extend to the Inferno.

The job ended in 1541. In 1564, on the 18th of February, Michael Angelo died and after the Council of Trent, during that same year, it was decided to cover some figures considered obscene. The commission for painting the coverings was granted to Daniele da Volterra, a disciple of the great artists, who was nicknamed *braghettone* ("big underwear"). He was not the only one, since in subsequent centuries the practice went ahead.

During the recent restorations of 1980-94, the doubt arose whether they should be removed, and the removal of the loincloths was decided upon, except for those of the main figures. Together with these restorations the luminous tones of the colours were also restored to what they were at the start, they having been

St Bartholomew displaying his flayed skin (a self-portrait by Michelangelo)

coated by the smoke from candles but also by a thin layer of paint having an animal glue that was laid on the vault during the 1710 restoration.

The painting decoration of the walls is broken down into three bands: in the lower part there are fake painted tapestries; in the center scenes from the Old and New Testaments, with scenes from the lives of Moses and Christ, and, above, portraits of the martyred popes.

The wall to the left of the last Judgement

The Baptism of Christ, *by Pietro Perugino*

In the river Jordan, John the Baptist baptizes Jesus. Descending from the sky is the dove of the Holy Spirit, sent by the Father, flanked by seraphim, cherubim and angels in flight. In the landscape are glimpsed an arch of triumph, the Colosseum and the Pantheon. To the left the Baptist preaching to the crowd, to the right Jesus doing the same thing. On both sides are portrayed contemporary personages.

The Temptations of Christ

The Temptations of Christ, *by Sandro Botticelli*

Above to the left Christ meets the Devil, who has the semblance of a hermit who invites him to transform stones into bread. In the center, against the background of a temple that takes up the form of the hospital of the Holy Spirit in Sassia (the hospital that stands between Rome's Borgo Santo Spirito and the Tiber) the Devil invites Jesus to throw himself into the void and be saved by his angels. To the right, Christ has the Devil fall from a cliff. In the foreground a sacrificial rite offered by a leper after having been restored to health by Christ.

Self-portrait by Botticelli

The Vocation of The First Apostles

Self-portrait by Ghirlandaio

The Vocation Of The First Apostles, *by Domenico Ghirlandaio*

In the center, a great lake with Jesus surrounded by his apostles, to the sides a multitude of spectators portraying the Florentine community in Rome.

The Sermon on the Mount *by Cosimo Rosselli*

Christ descends from Mount Sinai followed by the apostles and delivers his sermon to the crowds. To the left, a crowd listens to the sermon and in the background a city

The Sermon on the Mount

The Consignment of the Keys

immersed in a luxuriant landscape. To the right the healing of the leper by Jesus, surrounded by a crowd that depicts contemporary personages.

The Consignment of the Keys, *by Pietro Perugino*

The background for the group in the forefront is formed of a floor in perspective with at its center a typical Renaissance temple, with at the sides two arches of triumph. In the group to the right the man dressed in black gazing at the spectator is probably Perugino's self-portrait.

Evocation of the transfer of Christ's spiritual power to St. Peter and his successors.

The Last Supper, *by Cosimo Rosselli and Biagio d'Antonio*

A classical representation of the theme, with the special feature, inserted in the window, of the representation of the three episodes of the Passion: the Prayer in the garden, the capture of Christ, and the Crucifixion, attributed to Biagio d'Antonio.

Self-portrait by Perugino

The Vault

1. God Dividing Light from Darkness.
2. Creation of the Sun and the Moon.
3. God Separating Waters from the Land.
4. The Creation of Man.
5. The Creation of Woman.
6. The Originai Sin.
7. The Sacrifice of Noah.
8. The Deluge.
9. The Drunkennes of Noah.
10. The child Solomon with his mother.
11. The Parents of the future King.
12. The child Rehoboam with his mother. In the background, Solomon.
13. The child Asa with his father and his mother.
14. The child Uzziah with his mother and father Joram, and one of his brothers.
15. The child Ezekias with his mother, and father Ahaz.
16. The child Zorubabel with his mother, and his father Shealtiet.
17. The child Josiah with his mother and his father Amon.
18. The Prophet Jonah.
19. The Prophet Jeremiah.
20. The Prophet Daniel.
21. The Prophet Ezekiel.
22. The Prophet Isaiah.
23. The Prophet Joel.
24. The Prophet Zechariah.
25. The Libyan Sibyl.
26. The Persian Sibyl.
27. The Cumaean Sibyl.
28. The Erythrean Sibyl.
29. The Delphic Sibyl.
30. The Punishment of Haman.
31. The Brazen Serpent.
32. David and Goliath.
33. Judith and Holofernes

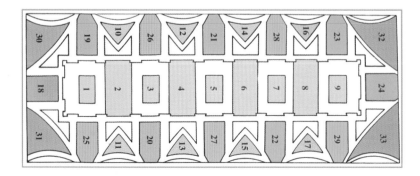

1. God Dividing Light from Darkness.
2. Creation of the Sun and the Moon.
3. God Separating Waters from the Land.
4. The Creation of Man.
5. The Creation of Woman.
6. The Originai Sin.
7. The Sacrifice of Noah.
8. The Deluge.
9. The Drunkennes of Noah.
10. The child Solomon with his mother.
11. The Parents of the future King.
12. The child Rehoboam with his mother. In the background, Solomon.
13. The child Asa with his father and his mother.
14. The child Uzziah with his mother and father Joram, and one of his brothers.
15. The child Ezekias with his mother, and father Ahaz.
16. The child Zorubabel with his mother, and his father Shealtiet.
17. The child Josiah with his mother and his father Amon.
18. The Prophet Jonah.
19. The Prophet Jeremiah.
20. The Prophet Daniel.
21. The Prophet Ezekiel.
22. The Prophet Isaiah.
23. The Prophet Joel.
24. The Prophet Zechariah.
25. The Libyan Sibyl.
26. The Persian Sibyl.
27. The Cumaean Sibyl.
28. The Erythrean Sibyl.
29. The Delphic Sibyl.
30. The Punishment of Haman.
31. The Brazen Serpent.
32. David and Goliath.
33. Judith and Holofernes

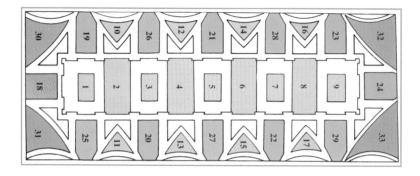

DELPHICA

Wall to the right of the last Judgement

Moses' trip into Egypt   *by Pietro Perugino*

Moses leaves for Egypt; an angel stops him, asking him to circumcise a woman's son, Eliezer. His mother Zipporah sees to the ceremony. In all the frescoes Moses is always portrayed with a gilded vestment and a green mantle.

Moses' Tests

Moses' Tests, *by Sandro Botticelli*

Moses kills an Egyptian who had mistreated a Jew. He combats the shepherds who want to keep the daughters of Jethro from letting their flocks drink in the pool. Moses removes his footwear and nears the briar, where he receives from God the mission to return into Egypt to free his people and lead them to the Promised Land.

The Punishment Of The Rebels

The Passage Through The Red Sea,
attributed to Domenico Ghirlandaio and Cosimo Rosselli

Moses and Aaron supplicate the pharaoh to free the people of Israel. God sends the ten plagues that induce the pharaoh to grant this but he instead decides to follow them with his army; the waters open that save the Jews and, closing back annihilate the Egyptian army. God strikes the Egyptian city with a flood.

The Punishment Of The Rebels *by Sandro Botticelli*

God punishes those who have rebelled against Moses and Aaron. During the voyage to the promised land the earth opens beneath their feet and swallows them and all their belongings; Joshua saves Moses from being stoned by the rebels and in the background of the scene the arch of Constantine is glimpsed. An allegorical evocation of the consequences of disobedience to the pope as the earthly representative of divine power.

Moses brings the tables

Having descended from Mount Sinai, *by Cosimo Rosselli*

Moses, kneeling on the mountain, accompanied by Joshua, receives the tables of the Law from God, surrounded by angels on a cloud. Moses brings the tables to the people of Israel, but discovers them adoring a golden calf, encouraged by Aaron. This scene provokes Moses' rage, and he throws the tables to the ground. In the background can be seen the punishment of the idolaters and the donation of new tables.

Moses' Testament And Death, *by Luca Signorelli and Bartolomeo della Gatta*

In the background Moses, on mount Nebo, receives from the angel the rod of command and with a gesture indicates the direction. To the left the death of Moses. In the foreground to the right he is speaking to the crowd, holding in his hand the rod and a book of holy scripture; to the left he gives the rod of command to Joshua.

Self-portrait
by Luca Signorelli